6.4   1pt

Quiz
151962

LEISURE

Information and projects to reduce your environmental footprint

Four Seasons Media Center

 **Marshall Cavendish Benchmark** New York

Helen Whittaker

This edition first published in 2012 in the United States of America by
Marshall Cavendish Benchmark
An imprint of Marshall Cavendish Corporation

Website: www.marshallcavendish.us

This publication represents the opinions and views of the author based on Helen Whittaker's personal experience, knowledge, and research. The information in this book serves as a general guide only. The author and publisher have used their best efforts in preparing this book and disclaim liability rising directly and indirectly from the use and application of this book.

Other Marshall Cavendish Offices:
Marshall Cavendish Ltd. 5th Floor, 32-38 Saffron Hill, London EC1N 8FH, UK • Marshall Cavendish International (Asia) Private Limited, 1 New Industrial Road, Singapore 536196 • Marshall Cavendish International (Thailand) Co Ltd. 253 Asoke, 12th Flr, Sukhumvit 21 Road, Klongtoey Nua, Wattana, Bangkok 10110, Thailand • Marshall Cavendish (Malaysia) Sdn Bhd, Times Subang, Lot 46, Subang Hi-Tech Industrial Park, Batu Tiga, 40000 Shah Alam, Selangor Darul Ehsan, Malaysia

Marshall Cavendish is a trademark of Times Publishing Limited

All websites were available and accurate when this book was sent to press.

Library of Congress Cataloging-in-Publication Data

Whittaker, Helen.
  Leisure / Helen Whittaker.
  p. cm. — (Living Green)
  Includes index.
  Summary: "Discusses how leisure activities impact the environment
  and what you can do to be more eco-conscious"—Provided by publisher.
  ISBN 978-1-60870-575-7
  1. Leisure—Environmental aspects—Juvenile literature. 2.
  Environmentalism—Juvenile literature. I. Title.
  GV45.W47 2012
790.1—dc22

                    2010044340

First published in 2011 by
MACMILLAN EDUCATION AUSTRALIA PTY LTD
15–19 Claremont Street, South Yarra 3141

Visit our website at www.macmillan.com.au or go directly to www.macmillanlibrary.com.au

Associated companies and representatives throughout the world.

Copyright © Macmillan Publishers Australia 2011

Publisher: Carmel Heron
Commissioning Editor: Niki Horin
Managing Editor: Vanessa Lanaway
Editor: Georgina Garner
Proofreader: Helena Newton
Designer: Julie Thompson
Page layout: Julie Thompson, Domenic Lauricella
Photo researcher: Claire Armstrong (management: Debbie Gallagher)
Illustrator: Cat MacInnes
Production Controller: Vanessa Johnson

Printed in China

Acknowledgments
The author and publisher are grateful to the following for permission to reproduce copyright material:

Front cover photograph: Girls shopping courtesy of Getty Images/John Lamb. Front and back cover illustrations by Cat MacInnes.

Photographs courtesy of: Corbis/Reed Kaestner, **13** (top), /moodboard, **16** (right), /Hans Neleman, **26**, /Louie Psihoyos, **10** (bottom), /Ariel Skelley, **9** (top), /TWPhoto, **6**; Getty Images/Chris Robbins, **8** (bottom); iStockphoto.com/Greg da Silva, **31**, /gchutka, **5**, /hartcreations, **22** (left), /Mark Hatfield, **13** (bottom), /photovideostock, **9** (bottom), /senorcampesino, **14** (top), /taekwondude, **14** (middle); Photolibrary/Alamy/Julio Etchart, **7** (top), /Alamy/Paris Market, **28**, /Alamy/Steve Skjold, **24**, /Polka Dot Images, **12** (top); Shutterstock/Akaiser, (environment icons, throughout), / John Austin, **11** (aeroplane), /V Borisov, **27**, /Katrina Brown, **4**, **32**, /Brenda Carson, **29**, /Jacek Chabraszewski, **12** (bottom), /Diego Cervo, **18**, / Mikael Damkier, **11** (bottom right), /devi, **11** (train), /Boris Diakovsky, **7** (bottom), /Edgewater Media, **11** (car), /Elena Elisseeva, **20**, /gsmad, **30** (middle), /Szasz-Fabian Ilka Erika, **3**, **22** (right), /jennyt, **11** (bus), /Laenz, (eco icons, throughout), /Olga Lyubkina, **8** (top), **15** (right), maxstockphoto, **9** (middle), /mmaxer, **30** (top), /Monkey Business Images, **14** (bottom), /Morgan Lane Photography, **10** (top), **15** (left), /Huguette Roe, **7** (middle), /saje, **12** (middle), /Charles Taylor, **16** (left), /Tool Using Animal, **11** (ship), /wrangler, **11** (top right), /Ye, (recycle logos, throughout), /Jin Young Lee, **30** (bottom).

While every care has been taken to trace and acknowledge copyright, the publisher tenders their apologies for any accidental infringement where copyright has proved untraceable. They would be pleased to come to a suitable arrangement with the rightful owner in each case.

Please note
At the time of printing, the Internet addresses appearing in this book were correct. Owing to the dynamic nature of the Internet, however, we cannot guarantee that all these addresses will remain correct.

1 3 5 6 4 2

Contents

Make hoops that don't harm the environment!
page 22

Glossary Words

When a word is printed in **bold**, you can look up its meaning in the Glossary on page 31.

Shop without any money at all! page 28

Living Green

Living green means choosing to care for the **environment** by living in a sustainable way.

Living Sustainably

Living sustainably means living in a way that protects Earth. Someone who lives sustainably avoids damaging the environment or wasting resources so that Earth can continue to provide a home for people in the future.

You and your friends can change your habits and behavior to help Earth. Living green makes sense!

How Our Actions Affect the Environment

Human activities use up Earth's **natural resources** and damage the environment. Some natural resources are **renewable**, such as wind and water, and some are **nonrenewable**, such as the **fossil fuels coal** and **oil**.

As the world's population grows, people are using more water, which creates water shortages, and are causing water **pollution**. We are using more nonrenewable resources too, which are usually mined from the earth and then burned, causing **habitat** destruction and air pollution. People cannot continue to live and act the way they do now—this way of life is unsustainable.

What Is an Environmental Footprint?

A person's environmental footprint describes how much damage that person does to the environment and how quickly the person uses up Earth's resources. A person who protects the environment and does not waste resources has a light environmental footprint. A person who pollutes the environment and wastes resources has a heavy environmental footprint.

Leisure

Our leisure activities have an impact on the environment. Understanding the environmental effects of our leisure activities can help us make "greener" choices and live more sustainably.

How Leisure Activities Affect the Environment

Some leisure activities use a lot of electricity or natural resources, and create pollution or harm the environment. Most electricity is generated by burning fossil fuels, which uses up natural resources, pollutes the air, and releases **carbon dioxide**, a **greenhouse gas** that contributes to **global warming**. We can live more sustainably by reducing the time we spend doing these sorts of activities and increasing the time we spend on activities that harm the environment less or that actively care for the environment.

Where to Next?

• To find out how indoor and outdoor activities, travel, and shopping can all affect the environment, go to the "Background Briefing" section on page 6.
• To try out fun projects that will help you reduce your environmental footprint, go to the "Living Green Projects" section on page 16.

How Does Using A Television Affect the Environment?

Building a television has many negative effects on the environment, and using it each day also affects the environment.

Mining the Raw Materials

Most of the raw materials used to make televisions, such as plastics, are made from nonrenewable resources. Mining these resources harms the environment.

Building the Television

A lot of electricity is used to make a television. Most electricity is generated using fossil fuels.

Packaging and Transporting the Television

Televisions bought in one country have often been made in another. Most vehicles that transport them run on fossil fuels. Packaging such as cardboard, plastic, and polystyrene is thrown out as waste.

Watching Television or Playing Games on the Television

A television runs on electricity.

Indoor Leisure Activities

Even when you are inside listening to music you are having an impact on the environment. Popular indoor leisure activities such as watching television, playing computer games, talking on the phone, and reading can all affect the environment negatively.

The Environmental Impacts of Indoor Leisure Activities

Audiovisual devices, paper products, plastic toys, and devices that use batteries all have negative effects on the environment.

Audiovisual Devices

Televisions, computers, MP3 players, and cell phones are types of audiovisual devices. They affect the environment at every stage, from the raw materials they're made from to how they are disposed of at the end of their lives.

Factory workers put together cell phones in Tokyo, Japan. The phones will be transported around the world.

Effects of Cell Phones

Cell phones affect the environment when they are being made, used, and even after they have been thrown away.

Gathering Raw Materials for a Phone

Most of the raw materials used to **manufacture** cell phones come from nonrenewable resources.

Making the Cell Phone

A lot of electricity is used to manufacture a cell phone.

Packaging

Cell phone packaging creates garbage, some of which is not **biodegradable**.

Transport

Most cell phones are manufactured in Asia and then transported around the world. Most trucks, airplanes, and ships run on fossil fuels.

Using the Cell Phone

Cell phones run on batteries powered by electricity. Most electricity is generated by burning fossil fuels.

Disposal

Cell phone batteries contain harmful substances. If old cell phones are disposed of in **landfill**, they can pollute the environment.

Paper Products

Paper products, such as magazines, are manufactured from wood, which is a renewable resource. However, paper production is not very sustainable because it uses large amounts of energy and water, and **paper mills** create a lot of air and water pollution. Paper can be **recycled** once it has been used.

Plastic Toys

Most plastics are made from oil or **natural gas**, which are nonrenewable fossil fuels and are not biodegradable. When you throw away a plastic toy or its plastic packaging, the plastic can take hundreds of years to break down.

Millions of plastic toys are produced in factories each year. When the toys break, the plastic ends up buried in a landfill site for hundreds of years.

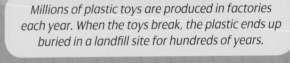

Battery-operated Devices

Making disposable batteries for devices such as radios uses up nonrenewable resources. When batteries are thrown out, **toxic** chemicals leak out of them and pollute the environment. Rechargeable batteries are more environmentally friendly. When they run out, they can be connected to an electrical charger, which restores their energy so they can be used again and again.

Outdoor Leisure Activities

Outdoor leisure activities such as hiking, camping, canoeing, and surfing are great fun, but be careful — if you aren't, you can damage the environment in all sorts of ways!

The Environmental Impacts of Outdoor Leisure Activities

Outdoor activities can have negative effects on the environment if you light fires, litter, or damage habitats.

Campfires are great fun, but they can have a disastrous effect on the environment if they get out of control.

Campfires

Campfires can get out of control and lead to wildfires, which can be disastrous for habitats, wildlife, and people who live nearby. Only adults should light fires and fires should never be left unattended. If a wildfire warning is in place, no one should light a fire. Take an electric camping stove instead.

Don't pick wildflowers. Even picking just a few flowers can damage a habitat and affect the animals and plants that live there.

Littering

Litter not only looks terrible, but many types of litter, such as empty cans, plastic bags, and broken bottles, can harm local wildlife. When you are getting ready to go hiking, camping, or picnicking, make sure you pack an extra bag so you can properly dispose of your trash.

Habitat Damage

Every living thing in a habitat relies on every other living thing for its survival. Picking flowers and taking other things from nature damages the natural habitat. Leave things the way you find them. Take photos, not flowers and rocks, to remind you of what you saw.

ECO FACT

About 100,000 marine mammals die every year from eating or becoming entangled in plastic. This plastic litter is washed from city streets into gutters and rivers and carried into the ocean.

Travel

Lots of people enjoy traveling in their free time. Whether you are going on a day trip or traveling abroad on vacation, the way that you choose to travel has an effect on the environment.

Manufacturing airplanes requires a lot of electricity, most of which is generated by burning fossil fuels. It also uses up natural resources, many of which are nonrenewable.

The Environmental Impacts of Travel

Travel affects the environment through the manufacture of different types of vehicles and the building of **infrastructure**. Also, most vehicles run on fossil fuels.

Manufacturing Vehicles

Manufacturing vehicles uses lots of energy and natural resources. It takes a lot more energy and resources to build a large vehicle, such as a passenger train, than a smaller vehicle, such as a car. But a train travels hundreds of miles and carries hundreds of people each day, so overall it may be more **energy efficient** than a car.

Building Infrastructure

Infrastructure for transportation includes roads, railways, parking lots, bus stations, railway stations, and airports. Building travel infrastructure uses a lot of natural resources and energy. It also takes up land that was previously home to plants and animals.

Burning Vehicle Fuel

Cars, buses, trains, ships, and airplanes all run on fuels made from the fossil fuel oil. Their engines burn the fuel, releasing greenhouse gases and other pollutants.

When people travel inefficiently, they burn more fossil fuel than needed. If four people travel to the same place in two different vehicles, they will burn much more fuel and have a larger environmental impact than if they traveled together in just one vehicle.

Fuel Burned by Different Types of Vehicles

Vehicle		Number of gallons (liters) of fuel burned to carry one passenger 60 miles (100 kilometers)
Passenger train		0.15–0.30 gallons (0.5–1 liters)
Bus		0.4 g (1.5 l)
Four-wheel drive car		0.6–1.5 g (2.5–5.5 l)
Passenger aircraft		1.25 g (4.5 l)
Cruise ship		3.5 g (13 l)

ECO FACT

Airplanes release their pollution high up in the sky, where it does more harm to the atmosphere than pollution released at ground level.

Shopping

When we shop for fun, we buy nonessential items, which are things that we want but do not need. Leisure purchases might be clothes, jewelry, or electronic goods.

Christmas shopping is an example of recreational spending. Most people buy gifts for each other that are usually things that they want — or don't want! — rather than things they need.

The Environmental Impacts of Shopping

Recreational shopping affects the environment because the goods need to be manufactured and transported, which uses energy and creates garbage. Stores and shopping centers also use a lot of energy.

Manufacturing and Transporting Goods

Manufacturing processes create garbage, which contributes to pollution. Manufacturing and transporting goods requires electricity, which usually comes from burning fossil fuels. This harms the environment and is not sustainable. The goods we buy and the packaging they come in use up natural resources. Some of these resources are nonrenewable.

ECO FACT

According to a survey, British children receive an average of ten Christmas presents each. Of these, 41 percent are broken within three months, and most end up as landfill.

Shopping Malls

Indoor shopping malls are popular places to go shopping. They have a negative environmental impact because they use more energy for lighting, heating, and cooling than outdoor shopping strip malls.

Internet Shopping

Millions of people shop online. This eliminates the need for some indoor shopping malls and strip malls, but because people can buy from all over the world, goods often need to be transported long distances. Transporting goods burns fossil fuels.

Shopping malls are popular places to shop, but they use more energy than outdoor shopping strips.

ECO FACT

The most popular items bought over the Internet are:
- books
- clothing, accessories, and shoes
- videos, DVDs, and games
- airline tickets
- electronic equipment

Four Seasons Media Center

What Can You Do?

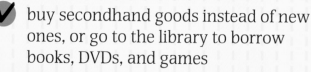

You can do many things to reduce the environmental impact of your leisure activities. Start with making sustainable choices about how to spend your free time.

Take unwanted electronic goods for recycling, so they will not be thrown out as waste and cause pollution.

Green Tips for Leisure Activities

For indoor leisure activities:

✓ take old electronic goods for recycling

✓ pay to download music and films online instead of buying CDs and DVDs

✓ do puzzles online instead of buying puzzle books

For outdoor leisure activities:

✓ take your litter home with you

✓ take nothing from nature except photographs

✗ do not light fires

When traveling for leisure:

✓ take a train or a bus rather than an airplane, if possible. Trains and buses produce much less pollution per passenger than cars and airplanes.

✓ for short journeys, walk, cycle, take public transportation, or arrange a car pool with friends

When shopping:

✓ buy secondhand goods instead of new ones, or go to the library to borrow books, DVDs, and games

✓ swap unwanted clothes and toys with friends

✗ avoid buying things you do not need

✗ do not buy things that have lots of packaging

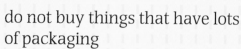

Leisure Activities that Benefit the Environment

Some leisure activities actively benefit the environment. You could join your local conservation volunteers, or you could set up your own project to improve some part of the local environment. For example, you could turn a corner of your backyard or schoolyard into a garden that attracts and provides a home for native wildlife.

Living Green Ratings and Green Tips

Pages 16–29 are filled with fun projects that will entertain you and help you protect Earth from waste and pollution.

Each project is given its own Living Green star rating— from zero to five—as a measurement of how much the project lightens your environmental footprint.

Some projects give Green Tips telling you how you can improve the project's Living Green rating even more.

Green Tip

To improve the Living Green rating, make the strap from an old belt or a bicycle inner tube.

On each project spread, look for the Living Green rating. Five stars is the highest—and greenest—rating!

Living Green Rating
★ ★ ★ ★ ★

★ ★ ★	★ ★ ★ ★	★ ★ ★ ★ ★
A three-star project will teach you about an issue and explain how you are wasting natural resources or causing pollution.	A four-star project will show one or two ways to reduce garbage or pollution.	A five-star project will help you reduce garbage and pollution and actively protect the environment in many different ways.

Chocolate-Chip Gift

Bake cookies as a tasty gift

Next time a holiday or a birthday comes around,
why not make a gift instead of buying one?
Homemade gifts are usually greener than store-
bought gifts and making them can be fun, too.

What You Need

- 9 ounces (250 grams) butter, softened
- 1 cup superfine sugar
- 1-1/2 cups soft brown sugar
- 2 eggs
- 2 teaspoons vanilla extract
- 1-1/2 teaspoons **baking soda**
- 1/2 teaspoon salt
- 3 teaspoons hot water
- 3-1/4 cups plain flour
- 13 oz. (375 g) chocolate chips
- Baking tray
- Baking paper

What to Do

1. Preheat the oven to 350°F (180°C).

2. Mix together the butter and both sugars until smooth.

3. Stir in the eggs, one at a time, until mixed.

4. Stir in the vanilla extract.

Save money and help save Earth by baking
a chocolate-chip gift for a friend.

5. Dissolve the baking soda and salt in the hot water, and then add to the mixture.

6. Stir in the flour and the chocolate chips.

7. Line a baking tray with baking paper.

Ask an adult for help when using the oven

8. Drop tablespoons of the mixture onto the baking paper.

9. Bake for about ten minutes, and then take them out of the oven, and wait for them to cool.

Green Tip

To improve the Living Green rating, wrap this gift in **recycled** paper and add a recycled bow (pages 18–19).

Recycled Wrapping Bow

Decorate gifts using old newspapers and magazines

Wrapping paper, bows, and cards are often thrown away immediately. If you reuse materials to decorate your gifts, you'll help save the environment from waste — and you'll save some money, too!

What You Need

• Old newspapers or magazines
• Scissors
• Stapler
• Adhesive tape
• Glue

What to Do

1. Cut four long strips of paper from a newspaper or magazine. Each strip should be the same length.

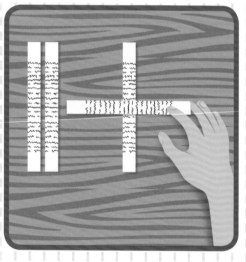

2. Place two of the strips so that they form a cross.

3. Fold the two ends of one strip into the middle. Hold in place.

Use old newspapers to create your own wrapping style.

4. Fold the two ends of the other strip into the middle, too. Staple both strips in place.

5. Repeat steps 2. to 4. with the other two strips of paper.

6. To form the bow, place one of the folded crosses on top of the other and staple in place.

7. Cut a small, round piece of newspaper or magazine. This will be the center of the bow.

8. Glue the center piece in place.

9. Add to a wrapped present and give to a friend!

Green Tip

Make other kinds of wrapping by reusing waste materials. You could:
• tie packages using old string, wool, or ribbon scraps
• make new gift tags from old birthday or holiday cards
• stamp or paint old newspaper to make one-of-a-kind paper

Music for the World

Make a conga drum from waste materials

If you like making music, create your own musical instruments that do not harm the environment. This drum sounds good and looks great. It is also sustainable because it uses waste materials.

What You Need

- Hacksaw
- Cardboard carpet or fabric tube
- Old plastic flowerpot with a base the same width as the carpet tube
- Two-piece plastic embroidery hoop that fits the top of the flowerpot
- Old beach ball or inflatable pool toy
- Duct tape
- Scissors
- Scrap paper
- Glue
- String

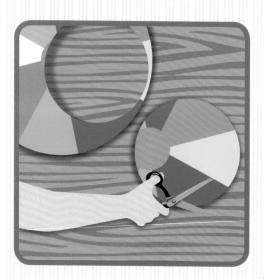

What to Do

1. Cut out a circle of plastic from the beach ball or inflatable pool toy. The circle should be big enough to fit over the embroidery hoop, plus an inch or so more.

2. Take the embroidery hoop apart. Place the circle of plastic over the inner hoop.

3. Keeping the plastic stretched tight, place the outer hoop over the plastic and inner hoop. This will be your drum head.

You can reuse materials from an old toy, such as an old beach ball, to create a new toy, such as a drum.

4. Place the drum head on top of the flowerpot and secure it with duct tape.

5. Using the hacksaw, cut a length of cardboard tube about one foot (30 cm) long.

Ask an adult to handle the hacksaw and cut the tube !

6. Use more duct tape to attach the base of the flowerpot to one end of the tube.

7. To hide the duct tape, wind string around it. Glue the string in place.

8. Decorate your drum by gluing on scraps of paper. Make some noise!

Green Tip

Ask your local carpet or fabric store for a cardboard tube. It will keep them from throwing it away.

Handmade Hoop

Make a mini-basketball hoop from waste materials

This mini-basketball hoop is fun to make and use. It's made from waste materials, so it allows you to practice your skills while you care for the environment.

Living Green Rating

★ ★ ★ ★

- Reduces the need to buy a manufactured hoop, so less environmental impact
- Sports do not usually use up nonrenewable resources or harm the environment
- Reduces landfill, because the netting and the old wallpaper are not thrown out as garbage

What You Need

- Large cardboard box
- Ruler
- Scissors
- Metal coat hanger
- Duct tape
- Old wallpaper
- Netting bag, such as a netted fruit bag
- Plastic embroidery hoop

What to Do

1. Cut out a square of cardboard about 1.3 feet (40 cm) along each side.

2. Use the wallpaper to cover one side of the cardboard.

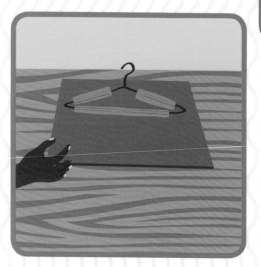

3. Place the coat hanger on the other side of the cardboard, as shown in the illustration. Hold it down with duct tape.

If you love basketball, help Earth by making your own hoop from waste materials.

4. Twist the coat hanger hook so that the end of the hook is pointing toward you.

5. Cut the top and bottom off the netting bag.

6. Fold the netting in half so that both open ends are at the bottom.

7. Open the embroidery hoop. Place the folded end of the netting inside the large hoop, just overlapping the hoop.

8. Put the embroidery hoop back together, trapping the netting.

9. Cut a slit through the cardboard where you want the hoop to go. The slit should be about 2 inches (5 cm) wide.

10. Place the hoop through the slit. Secure it in place at the back, using two strips of duct tape.

11. Hang your completed basketball hoop over a door. Shoot some hoops!

Green Tip

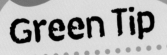

Make some environmentally friendly "balls" to use with your hoop. Try:
- scrunched-up newspaper
- balled-up socks
- plastic bags bound together with rubber bands

Striped for Speed

Update your bike by adding racing stripes

Cycling is a clean and sustainable form of transport. By giving your bike a makeover, you can make it more fun to ride, which might mean you use it more often.

What You Need

- An old bike
- Wrench
- Soap or detergent
- Warm water
- Bucket
- Old sponge
- Old towel
- Plastic wrap
- Newspaper
- Overalls
- Rubber gloves
- Goggles
- Gas or fume mask
- Masking tape
- Scissors
- Spray paints in silver and black

If your bike is looking a bit old, why not give it a face-lift?

What to Do

1. Put your bike outside and turn it upside down. Using the wrench, remove the wheels.

2. Wash the bike's paintwork with the old sponge soaked in a mixture of soap and warm water.

3. Rinse, and then dry with an old towel.

4. Place newspaper underneath the bike.

5. Use plastic wrap to cover the parts of your bike that you do not want painted, such as the seat, handlebars, and pedals.

6. Put on the overalls, rubber gloves, goggles, and the gas or fume mask. This will protect you from the paint and its fumes.

7. Spray your bike's paintwork silver. Leave to dry.

8. Use a pair of scissors to cut masking tape into narrow strips.

9. When the silver paint is dry, apply strips of masking tape to where you want silver lines on your bike.

10. Spray your bike's paintwork black.

11. When the black paint is completely dry, peel off the masking tape and you'll see your silver stripes. Try out your new bike!

Other Design Ideas

Try these other design ideas for your bicycle makeover:

• paint your bike in the colors of your favorite sports team
• use a sponge to apply splotches of paint in browns and greens, creating a camouflage style
• use an old toothbrush to splatter different colored paints, such as red, yellow, and blue

Green Tip

Fit your bike with a basket or a trailer. You can then cycle to the shops you like instead of having an adult drive you.

Nature Watch Diary

Watch what's happening in your local environment

A nature watch project helps you learn about your local environment by watching and taking note of local wildlife, plants, and weather. Over time, you may begin to notice patterns in the types of things you see.

What You Need

• Notebook
• Pens
• Pencils
• Ruler
• Camera (optional)
• Photo printer (optional)
• Glue (optional)

What to Do

1. Ask your friends or classmates if they would like to join you in starting a nature-watch group, or start watching by yourself.

2. Use your local library and the Internet to research local wildlife and plants. This will help you recognize what you see.

3. Choose a location from which to observe. This could be a local park, your backyard, or your schoolyard. Make sure that the location has lots of native plants. These plants will attract animals, birds or insects.

4. Create a nature-watch diary by making tables on each page of your notebook. See the example table on page 27.

5. Start watching. Try to make your observations at different times each day.

Watching birds come and go in your garden can help you appreciate nature and your local area.

Sample Nature Watch Diary Page

Name: Stevie Wu

Date	Weather	Observations	Location
Sept 29, 2012	Sunny, with afternoon rain	Small yellow flowers beginning to open up (need to identify)	Local park, Greentown
		About ten bats flying overhead in the early evening	
Sept 30, 2012	Sunny	One large green frog (see sketch) in pond in early morning	Local park, Greentown
Oct 1, 2012	Cloudy	Two frogs in park today, and a small bird feeding in a tree (see photo)	Local park, Greentown, and backyard, Greentown
		About twenty bats flying over backyard about 7 P.M.	

Green Tip

Find out if your area is covered by a local nature-watch organization. These organizations collect the information recorded by local people and add it to a large database.

6. Fill in your diary each day with notes about the animals and plants you see and how they behave. Make sure you note the date, weather, and location. Make sketches of the things you see or take photographs, print them, and glue them into your diary.

7. Try to identify all the animals and plants you see. Compare your notes with those of other nature watchers.

Swap Meet Treasures

Swap books, games, and clothes with your friends

Rather than buying brand-new books, games, and clothes, hold a swap meet with your friends and see what treasure you can find. You can exchange things you no longer want for things that you've always wanted.

Living Green Rating

★ ★ ★ ★

- Reduces the need to buy brand-new, manufactured things, so less environmental impact
- Reduces landfill, because the old books, games, and clothes are not thrown out as garbage

What You Need

- An area with a large table to spread everything out on
- Old cardboard boxes
- Poster paper
- Thin cardboard, such as old cereal boxes
- Scissors
- Hole punch
- String
- Felt-tip pens
- Paper
- Pens

What to Do

1. Get together with your friends and suggest a swap meet.

2. Decide on the date that you will hold the swap meet and where it will be. A sheltered outside area would be perfect in any weather.

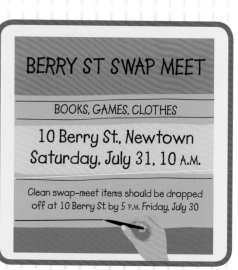

BERRY ST SWAP MEET

BOOKS, GAMES, CLOTHES

10 Berry St., Newtown
Saturday, July 31, 10 A.M.

Clean swap-meet items should be dropped off at 10 Berry St by 5 P.M. Friday, July 30

3. Make posters to advertise the swap meet (see example poster). The poster should invite people to gather their unwanted books, games, or clothes and drop them off the night before. Ask your teacher if you can hang the posters at school.

4. When someone drops off items, put their things in a box and write the person's name on the box.

Remember the saying "One person's trash is another person's treasure!" You might find many treasures at a swap meet.

5. Create name tags, so that during the swap meet you'll remember who brought each item. To make a tag, cut a shape from the thin cardboard and write the person's name on it.

6. Punch a hole in each name tag and thread string through the hole.

7. Attach a tag to each item using the string. For a book, just place a tag within its pages.

8. On the morning of the swap meet, lay out all the items on the table.

9. Once everyone has arrived, start to swap!

Find Out More About Living Green

The Internet is a great way of finding out more about how leisure activities affect the environment and what you can do to make more sustainable leisure choices.

Useful Websites

Visit these useful websites:

www.arkive.org
This website has information about endangered animals all around the world. You can search by location, contribute your own photos, and play online games.

http://eartheasy.com/play_bkyd_wildhab.htm
This web page gives instructions for turning part of your backyard into a home for animals, insects, and birds.

http://unep.org/tunza/children
This website from the United Nations has downloadable fact sheets about environmental issues, tips for living more sustainably, and competitions you can enter.

Searching for Information

Here are some terms you might enter into your Internet search bar to find out more about leisure and the environment:
- recycling electronic waste
- environmental impact of plastic
- human-powered vehicles
- eco-friendly products

Glossary

audiovisual devices Sources of information and forms of entertainment that play sound and show pictures.

baking soda White, powdery chemical compound used for cooking and cleaning; also called sodium bicarbonate or bicarb soda.

biodegradable Able to rot away or be broken down naturally without harming the environment.

carbon dioxide A greenhouse gas that is released when fossil fuels are burned, for example when coal is burned to make electricity.

energy efficient Using a small amount of energy compared to other similar items.

environment The natural world, including plants, animals, land, rivers, and oceans.

fossil fuels Coal, oil, and natural gas, which are natural resources that are formed from remains of dead plants and animals, deep under Earth's surface, over millions of years.

global warming The process by which Earth's average temperature is getting warmer.

greenhouse gases Gases, such as carbon dioxide or water vapor, that trap the heat of the sun in Earth's atmosphere.

habitat Place where plants and animals live.

infrastructure Structures and buildings, such as roads, railways, and airports, needed for some kind of system to operate.

landfill Garbage that is buried and covered with soil at garbage dumps.

manufacture Make from raw materials into a product for people to buy and use.

natural gas A gas found underground, often with other fossil fuels such as coal and petroleum; it is mainly made up of methane.

natural resources Natural materials that can be used by people, such as wood, metal, coal, and water.

nonrenewable resources Natural resources that cannot be easily replaced, such as coal, oil, and natural gas.

oil A liquid found in rocks, formed from the remains of plants and animals that lived millions of years ago.

paper mills Factories where trees are turned into paper.

pollution Damaging substances, especially chemicals or waste products, that harm the environment.

recycled Having treated the materials contained in a product so that they can be used again.

renewable resources Natural resources that will never run out, such as the wind, or that can easily be replaced, such as wood.

toxic Poisonous to living things.

Index